Original title:
Whirlwinds of Wonder and Zzz's

Copyright © 2024 Creative Arts Management OÜ
All rights reserved.

Author: Oliver Bennett
ISBN HARDBACK: 978-9916-90-526-5
ISBN PAPERBACK: 978-9916-90-527-2

The Dance of Drowsiness

In the twilight's gentle sway,
Dreams begin their soft ballet,
Whispers wrap the world in gray,
As night steals the day away.

Eyes grow heavy, thoughts subdued,
In this calm, a peaceful mood,
Stars appear, a silver brood,
As shadows dance, the heart's renewed.

Tornado of Thoughts

Thoughts collide like stormy gales,
Twisting visions, vivid trails,
In the chaos, a heart sails,
Seeking peace where silence prevails.

Mind like lightning, fierce and bright,
Chasing whispers through the night,
Yearning for a still delight,
In the whirlwind, find the light.

Breezy Bedtime Tales

Once upon a moonlit sea,
Waves of dreams call out to me,
In the breezy, soft decree,
Adventures swim, wild and free.

Stars twinkle with stories old,
Tales of bravery unfold,
In the night, where dreams are sold,
Imagination's treasure told.

Serene Swirls of Night

Night descends with colors deep,
In its arms, the world will sleep,
With a sigh, the secrets keep,
In the calm, the shadows sweep.

Moonlight dances, soft and bright,
Guiding dreams with gentle light,
As the stars, like diamonds, write,
Stories woven into night.

Chasing the Zephyrs

In fields of gold, we run and chase,
Soft winds embrace, a gentle grace.
The laughter dances in the air,
As carefree hearts have not a care.

Through valleys deep, and mountains high,
We follow dreams that soar and fly.
Each whispered breeze, a sweet delight,
Guiding us to the fading light.

Reverie in the Tempest

Amid the storm, our spirits rise,
With thunder's roar, we touch the skies.
The tempest howls, yet we find peace,
In chaos, our fears begin to cease.

Raindrops dance on window panes,
In swirling winds, we break our chains.
A symphony of wild embrace,
Where heartbeats find their rightful place.

Whispers of the Twirling Clouds

Upon the breeze, soft secrets soar,
The clouds converse, a calming roar.
In hues of gray and ivory white,
They share their tales, both day and night.

With every shift, a story told,
Of sunlit dreams and nights so bold.
They twist and twirl, a silent dance,
Inviting us to take a chance.

Driftwood Dreams

Upon the shore, the driftwood lies,
Each piece a tale beneath the skies.
Carved by time, and waves' caress,
In silence, they hold their quiet stress.

With every grain, a memory made,
Of stormy nights and sunlit glades.
We gather them, our hearts aligned,
In driftwood dreams, our souls entwined.

Odes of Dusk and Dawn

The sun dips low, the shadows grow,
A canvas stained in fiery glow.
Whispers of night begin to weave,
As twilight bids the day to leave.

Stars emerge in velvet skies,
A moonlit dance, the world, it sighs.
With every breath, the evening stirs,
In hushed tones, the cosmos purrs.

Awake, the dawn, with golden light,
Chasing dreams of the quiet night.
Colors bloom in radiant hues,
A symphony, the day renews.

Dusk and dawn, a sacred space,
Time unfolds at a gentle pace.
In every glow, a tale is spun,
A bridge from dark to light begun.

The Ebb of Sleep's Enchantment

In twilight's arms, the world drifts slow,
Where quiet whispers begin to flow.
Dreams take flight on softest wings,
A realm where peace and silence clings.

Moonbeams dance on slumbering eyes,
In shadows cast, the heart complies.
A lullaby of sweet embrace,
Wrapped in time, a gentle grace.

Yet as dawn's whisper starts to rise,
The spell unravels, softly sighs.
The ebb of sleep, a fleeting chase,
Awakens hope in daylight's face.

In sleepy depths where visions wane,
Awaits the light, a soft refrain.
Though dreams may fade, their echoes persist,
In waking hours, they still exist.

Storms of Dreams

In the shadowed night, whispers call,
Winds of longing begin to stall.
Cascading thoughts, a tempest brew,
Chasing visions, lost in the blue.

Lightning strikes, illusions dance,
Hope flickers in a daring glance.
Clouds of desire drift far away,
Carried on dreams, come what may.

Tidal waves of silent screams,
Drowning softly in the beams.
Tempest hearts, set free to roam,
In storms of dreams, we find our home.

As twilight fades into the night,
Unseen sails catch moonlit light.
Journey through the windswept seams,
Lost forever in our dreams.

Vortex of Imagination

In the whirlpool of my mind,
Thoughts collide, entwined, unkind.
Colors swirl, a vivid shade,
Reality and dreams parade.

Echoes dance in spiraled form,
Ideas surge, a restless storm.
Boundless realms, a canvas bright,
Painting stars that pierce the night.

Whispers thread through inner space,
Constructing worlds, a daring race.
Cascading visions, time unmeasured,
In this vortex, dreams are treasured.

Dare to leap and lose control,
Dive into the depths of soul.
Here where fantasies ignite,
In the vortex, we take flight.

Slumbering Cyclones

Beneath the calm of moonlit skies,
Hush of night conceals the sighs.
Gentle breezes cradle the earth,
While slumbering cyclones whisper mirth.

Time stands still as shadows play,
Rippling dreams drift far away.
In the silence, secrets spin,
Winds of change, where hopes begin.

Softly swirling, visions blend,
In the stillness, fears suspend.
Cyclones rise without a sound,
In slumber's grasp, we're tightly bound.

Awake we rise, yet still they lie,
In hidden depths, we fear to fly.
Embrace the hope, let shadows wane,
For even storms can soothe the pain.

Fantasia in the Breeze

Whispers weave through branches high,
A dance of leaves, a lullaby.
Every flutter tells a tale,
Of drifting dreams on winds that sail.

Colors burst in vibrant flight,
As day gives way to velvet night.
Fantasia sings with airy grace,
Unfolding wonders, time and space.

Clouds drift lazily on the shore,
Carrying tales of yesteryore.
Through the breeze, a gentle tease,
In spirals of our soul's unease.

Catch the magic, let it flow,
In the breeze, let spirits grow.
Heartfelt wishes ride on air,
In the fantasia, without a care.

Flows of Serene Slumber

In twilight's hush, the dreams do weave,
Soft shadows dance, as hearts believe.
A gentle sigh, the night holds tight,
In flows of calm, we find our light.

The stars above begin to glow,
Whispers of peace in the night's soft flow.
Wrapped in warmth, the world fades slow,
In serene slumber, we softly go.

Currents of Enchantment

Beneath the moon, the ripples gleam,
Echoes of magic in the stream.
Waves of wonder, silence speaks,
In currents deep, our spirit seeks.

Through forest glades, the shadows play,
A dance of light in soft array.
Boundless hearts on journeys vast,
In enchantment's grip, we breathe our past.

Wanderlust Whispers

In the break of dawn, new paths await,
Whispers of wander, calling straight.
Footsteps eager, the world unfolds,
In stories woven, the brave and bold.

With every turn, the heart does race,
Chasing dreams in an endless space.
A journey sweet, alive with grace,
Wanderlust whispers in every place.

Trails of Sleepy Surprise

Through meadows soft, the shadows creep,
Beneath the skies, where secrets sleep.
Each gentle rustle, a lullaby,
On trails of calm, the heart will fly.

Bouquets of dreams in the morning mist,
Softly beckon, a tender twist.
With every step, the day ignites,
In sleepy surprise, the soul takes flight.

The Tangle of Soft Surroundings

In the garden where shadows play,
Whispers of color blend and sway.
Petals rest in gentle embrace,
Nature's art, a sacred space.

Leaves like laughter dance in the breeze,
Infused with warmth, they sway with ease.
Silent stories in the night,
The world wrapped in starlit light.

Around the brook, the soft moss grows,
Where tranquil melody softly flows.
In harmony, all beings blend,
In this haven, we transcend.

The sun dips low, a golden hue,
Soft surroundings hold secrets true.
In the tangle, we find our peace,
A refuge where worries cease.

Dancing Lights in Dusk

As twilight paints the evening sky,
Stars awaken, twinkling high.
Fireflies flicker, a lively dance,
In shadows deep, they take their chance.

The horizon blushes, dreams arise,
Moonlit whispers, night's disguise.
Branches sway and secrets come,
To greet the night, the day is done.

Waves of laughter fill the air,
Joyful hearts, a light to share.
With every twinkle, stories weave,
In dancing lights, we dare believe.

Embrace the dusk, let spirits soar,
In the magic, we crave for more.
In each glimmer, moments freeze,
A celestial waltz with gentle ease.

Chasing the Zephyrs of Sleep

As starlight spills upon the ground,
A hush envelops, dreams unbound.
Softly calling, the night winds sigh,
Lulling hearts as shadows fly.

Feathers float on whispering air,
Through the silence, a gentle care.
In the stillness, a lullaby glows,
Inviting peace, where freedom flows.

Memory dances on the breeze,
In slumbering moments, souls find ease.
Chasing whispers, we drift away,
To realms where dreams begin to play.

A moonlit smile, a fleeting touch,
In twilight's clutch, we sense so much.
Chasing zephyrs, in the deep,
We lose ourselves in the arms of sleep.

Spirited Adventures in Quietude

In a meadow where the wildflowers bloom,
A spirit stirs, dispelling gloom.
Nature beckons with open arms,
Whispers of wonder, softening charms.

With every step, the world unfolds,
A tapestry woven with stories told.
Hidden trails beneath the trees,
Inviting wonder on a gentle breeze.

Softly laughing, the brook flows near,
In its laughter, joys appear.
Adventures wait in silence deep,
Where vibrant dreams begin to leap.

In stillness, hearts can truly roam,
In quietude, we build our home.
Spirited journeys quietly guide,
In nature's embrace, we confide.

The Comet's Dream

Across the silent night, it glides,
A trail of stardust, where hope resides.
With whispers bright that light the dark,
Each sparkle gleams, igniting a spark.

Through realms of time, it weaves its flight,
A cosmic dance, a wondrous sight.
Carried forth by time's sweet stream,
The universe holds the comet's dream.

From fiery heart to icy tail,
It journeys forth, a bold detail.
In every glance, a wish takes form,
A fleeting moment, a cosmic storm.

As planets turn and stars align,
The comet sweeps, a grand design.
Within the night's soft, velvet seam,
It writes the stars, the comet's dream.

Drowsy Waves of Inspiration

Gentle tides roll in and sway,
With whispered thoughts that drift away.
In quiet moments, dreams arise,
Like floating clouds in endless skies.

The ocean's hum, a lullaby,
Carries hopes that never die.
Each wave a brush on canvas wide,
Where colors blend and dreams abide.

As seagulls dance on breezy trails,
Inspiration flows, as wind prevails.
The shoreline beckons, soft and true,
A tranquil space for thoughts anew.

In drowsy waves, we find our muse,
A soothing balm, we gladly choose.
With every crest and every fall,
We ride the tide, responding to the call.

Naps in Nebulas

Amidst the stars, a cradle swings,
In twilight's hush, where quiet sings.
The nebulas wrap in pastel hue,
A dreamy rest for hearts so true.

In swirls of light, we close our eyes,
Drifting through soft cosmic sighs.
With every breath, we start to feel,
A sense of peace that's almost real.

Galaxies whisper with gentle grace,
In this vast and wondrous space.
Floating dreams like paper boats,
Drifting softly where wonder floats.

Napping in pools of starlit streams,
We awaken slowly, lost in dreams.
The universe cradles us in embrace,
As we explore this magic place.

Celestial Curls of Calm

In twilight's hush, the stars unfurl,
Glimmers of light in a velvet swirl.
Each cosmic wave a soothing balm,
Awakening the soul, so calm.

As moonbeams weave through branches high,
A gentle touch that makes us sigh.
With every sparkle, dreams entwine,
In cosmic dances, hearts align.

Through silent whispers of the night,
Celestial curls bring pure delight.
A tapestry of peace and grace,
Erasing worries, filling space.

In this embrace, we find release,
A tranquil heart, a sense of peace.
Within the night, we lose our qualm,
In celestial curls, we find our calm.

Melodies of the Midnight Gale

Whispers dance in shadowed light,
Echoes play through silent night.
Stars like diamonds weave a tune,
Crickets sing beneath the moon.

Leaves are rustling in the trees,
Carried on a fragrant breeze.
Nature hums a soft refrain,
Lullabies of joy and pain.

Clouds drift slowly, soft and pale,
Guided by the midnight gale.
Hearts will wander, souls will sigh,
Lost in dreams as time slips by.

In the stillness, we find grace,
Melodies that time won't erase.
Every note a fleeting spark,
In the beauty, we leave a mark.

Flickering Dreams

In the quiet of the night,
Fragments shimmer, soft and light.
Glimmers dance upon the waves,
In our hearts, the wonder braves.

Shadows blend with hope and fear,
Flickering dreams, both far and near.
Chasing whispers in the dark,
Every thought ignites a spark.

Time stands still as visions play,
Woven thoughts that drift away.
Reality meets fantasy,
In the silence, we are free.

Life's a canvas, painted bright,
Filled with colors in the night.
Hold the dreams, and let them soar,
Flickering, they ask for more.

Ephemeral Twists of Fortune

Life's a game of chance and fate,
Paths entwine, we wait and rate.
Moments fleeting, like the breeze,
A twist of fate brings us to our knees.

Laughter mingles with despair,
Fortunes shift; they're never fair.
Like a river, flows the day,
Unpredictable in every way.

The stars align or drift apart,
Each decision a work of art.
In this dance, we learn to grow,
Embracing highs, enduring lows.

Time reveals the unexpected,
Lessons learned, and hearts connected.
With open minds, we shall explore,
Ephemeral, yet craving more.

Breezes through the Looking Glass

Through the looking glass we see,
Worlds that twist with mystery.
Breezes whisper, secrets shared,
In reflections, dreams are bared.

Time unfolds in colors bright,
Turning shadows into light.
Every glance, a portal wide,
Where imagination takes a ride.

Moments blend like fleeting dew,
Each new glance brings something new.
In this realm of what might be,
Boundless visions set us free.

So we venture, hearts aglow,
Through the glass, we come to know.
Every breath a chance to find,
Magic woven through the mind.

Nightfall in a Twirl

The sky wears a cloak, deep blue and dark,
Stars twinkle softly, each one a spark.
Whispers of wind curl through the trees,
Gentle and sweet like a lover's tease.

Shadows dance lightly on the soft ground,
Moonbeams weave paths where silence is found.
Crickets play tunes in the night's embrace,
While dreams take their flight in this tranquil space.

The Winged Incidents

Feathers flit by, in a sudden breeze,
Stories of journeys, whispered with ease.
Birds trace arcs against the blue sky,
In the fleeting moments, they soar high.

Fragments of light shimmer on their wings,
Echoes of laughter that soft morning brings.
Nature's canvas painted with grace,
Life unfolds gently in each wide space.

Elysian Dreams in Turbulence

In the heart of storms, colors collide,
Winds paint the skies, relentless they ride.
Clouds twist and churn, a wild ballet,
Yet hope flickers bright, lighting the way.

Amidst the chaos, a calm can be found,
Whispers of peace ripple through the sound.
Dreams intertwine with the powerful gale,
Elysian glimpses in the latest tale.

Whims of the Wandering Clouds

Clouds drift lazily, in their soft race,
Changing their forms, like a child's embrace.
Whispers of stories float high above,
Crafted in silence, each one a love.

As shadows stretch long, they dance on the ground,
Ballet of nature, a soft, gentle sound.
In the world below, they leave their trace,
Reminders of dreams in a vast, open space.

Touched by Cosmic Whirls

In the night sky, whispers play,
Galaxies twirl, in endless sway.
Stars align, a dance divine,
Hearts beat softly, mystery's sign.

Dreamers gaze, their spirits soar,
Through the void, they seek for more.
With every spark, a tale unfolds,
In cosmic arms, the universe holds.

Nebulas paint in vibrant hues,
Guiding souls with lighted views.
Time drifts gently, boundless space,
Touched by whirls of cosmic grace.

In the silence, echoes bloom,
Lost in the vastness, thoughts consume.
Connected threads through cosmic art,
A timeless journey, heart to heart.

Starlight on a Whirl

Starlight glimmers on a swirl,
In the night, a tale unfurl.
Constellations weave their fate,
Mystic stories to relate.

Each twinkle holds a secret deep,
Silent vows, the heavens keep.
Waves of light through darkness spell,
Whispers soft, a magic well.

Planets spin in graceful arcs,
While dreams ignite like glowing sparks.
Along the path of fate we stroll,
Starlight dances, heart and soul.

Minds adrift in wonder's stream,
Caught within a waking dream.
Cosmic wonders fuel the fire,
Awakening a heart's desire.

Cosmic Currents of Calm

In the depths of endless night,
Cosmic currents flow with light.
Serenity wrapped in stars,
Welcoming peace from afar.

Gentle whispers ride the breeze,
Filling hearts with tender ease.
Every twinkle, every hue,
Sings a lullaby so true.

Time stands still, the cosmos breathes,
Holding dreams like autumn leaves.
In this space, we find our balm,
Drifting softly, feelings calm.

Bathe in the glow of the skies,
Let your spirit learn to rise.
In the cosmos, we embrace,
Currents of love, a warm grace.

Discoveries in a Daydream

In a daydream, worlds collide,
Horizons opened, visions wide.
Whispers of hope float on air,
Adventures bloom, beyond compare.

Thoughts meander like a stream,
Woven threads of every dream.
Curiosities take flight,
Dancing shadows greet the night.

With each glance, a story spun,
Colors blend until they're one.
Lost in wonder, hearts ignite,
Discoveries flourish, pure delight.

In this realm where time stands still,
Creative sparks begin to thrill.
A gateway into something new,
Daydreams guide us, bright and true.

Tangles of Twilight

In shadows deep, the whispers play,
Where dusk and dawn weave night and day.
The colors blend in gentle sighs,
As stars awaken in velvet skies.

The branches dance in twilight's grace,
Embracing light in a warm embrace.
A symphony of hues unfolds,
As night reveals its secrets bold.

In every corner, dreams ignite,
Caught in the web of fading light.
With every breath, the world sways slow,
In tangles where the twilight flows.

Hibernating Hues

Beneath the frost, the earth sleeps tight,
Swathed in blankets of moonlit white.
Colors fade into soft retreat,
In winter's grasp, where stillness meets.

Shadows linger in crisp, cool air,
As whispers fade with a gentle care.
Each breath is seen in clouds of hope,
In hibernation, the heart will cope.

Memories linger in silent dreams,
Where warmth will rise from icy streams.
The palette waits, a muted muse,
For spring's embrace and vibrant hues.

The Lull of the Luminous

In quiet still, the moonlight spills,
A lull that wraps the world in chills.
Soft glimmers dance on surface calm,
A whispering touch, a tranquil balm.

The stars compose a gentle tune,
A lullaby beneath the moon.
In every flicker, stories weave,
In luminous threads, we dare believe.

With every heartbeat, peace descends,
And in the dark, the light transcends.
In night's embrace, our spirits soar,
In the lull of radiant lore.

Threads of the Tranquil Tide

A gentle flow, the ocean sighs,
As moonlight spills across the skies.
Waves embrace in a rhythmic dance,
In threads of peace, the heart finds chance.

The shoreline whispers tales untold,
Of secrets deep and treasures bold.
Each grain of sand holds time's embrace,
In tranquil tides, we find our place.

Beneath the stars, the waters gleam,
In every wave, a fleeting dream.
The night unfolds in softest hues,
In threads of calm, we find our muse.

The Spirited Dancer

In a swirl of colors bright,
She twirls beneath the moonlight,
Every step a story spun,
Her spirit glows like morning sun.

The music whispers, soft and sweet,
Guiding her in graceful beat,
With every leap, she breaks the ground,
In a world where joy is found.

Her laughter dances through the air,
An echo of her soul laid bare,
With every spin, her heart takes flight,
A ballet star in the night.

Underneath the stars so wide,
She flows like waves upon the tide,
In her rhythm, dreams come alive,
The spirited dancer will always thrive.

Wonders Wrapped in Clouds

Floating dreams on gentlest breeze,
Whispers heard among the trees,
Colors blend in soft embrace,
Nature holds a sacred space.

Each cloud a canvas, light and free,
Painting scenes for all to see,
With dawn's kiss, they start to glow,
A moment lost, yet never slow.

The sky unravels secrets old,
In silver threads and shades of gold,
Wonder wrapped in every fold,
Stories waiting to be told.

Drifting on, they play their part,
A symphony to touch the heart,
In a dance, both soft and loud,
Life's wonders wrapped in clouds.

Swaying with the Sleepy Stars

As evening falls and shadows grow,
Stars begin their gentle show,
Whispers of the night unfold,
Stories in their light retold.

Swaying softly, dreams arise,
Painting wishes in the skies,
Each twinkle holds a secret song,
Inviting hearts to dream along.

Beneath the gaze of cosmic eyes,
Peace descends, and worries die,
In their glow, we find our place,
Lost in beauty, time we trace.

With every blink, a wish is made,
In the dance of stars, we're swayed,
And in the silence, we shall find,
The magic woven, hearts aligned.

Fantasies in Motion

In a realm where dreams ignite,
Fantasies take graceful flight,
Each idea a vibrant hue,
Painting life with wonders new.

With every turn, adventures call,
Echoes of the world enthrall,
In our hearts, a fire burns bright,
Chasing shadows, seeking light.

Moments blend and realities shift,
Imagination's sweetest gift,
A tapestry of hopes we weave,
In every sigh, we learn to believe.

Whispers guide our journey's course,
In every dream, we find our source,
With open hearts, we set in motion,
The magic's dance, a boundless ocean.

Spirals of Peace

In gardens where whispers grow,
Soft petals dance in gentle flow.
The sunbeams twirl in golden light,
Nature's embrace feels so right.

Breezes hum a soothing tune,
Beneath the watch of a friendly moon.
Rippling streams share tales of old,
In their depths, calm dreams unfold.

Silent woods, a sacred space,
Time slows down in this warm place.
Hearts find solace, spirits soar,
In every moment, peace at the core.

As night descends, stars gleam bright,
Guiding the way with silver light.
In spirals of peace, we remain,
United in joy, free from pain.

Secrets of the Calm Storm

In the hush before rain starts,
Nature speaks to restless hearts.
Clouds gather, a quilt of gray,
Whispers of wind lead the way.

Lightning's flash, a dance of light,
Thunder rumbles, a distant fight.
Yet within, the calm is near,
Secrets held for those who hear.

Raindrops fall, a tender kiss,
Nature's rhythm, a moment of bliss.
Every splash, a hidden spell,
In quietude, all is well.

Underneath this tempest's charm,
There's beauty found, a soothing balm.
For even storms have tales to share,
If we listen, we'll find them there.

Lullabies in the Gales

Winds weave tales of distant shores,
Gentle whispers, the world adores.
Underneath the skies that sway,
Lullabies guide the end of day.

Moonbeams dance on rippling seas,
Carrying soft, enchanting pleas.
In the chaos, hearts find home,
A melody where dreams can roam.

Every gust tells stories old,
Of brave souls and treasures untold.
In the gale, love's song prevails,
Cradled softly, in tender trails.

Close your eyes, let worries cease,
Embrace the calm, find your peace.
In lullabies of winds that call,
Feel the magic, embrace it all.

Naps in the Cyclone

Within the whirlwind's dizzy spin,
A sanctuary, quiet within.
Though chaos reigns, there's a charm,
In tempest's arms, we find our calm.

Raindrops tap like soothing hands,
A rhythm that the heart understands.
Pillows soft amidst the storm,
As dreams in swirling winds take form.

Moments dance like kite on string,
The heart finds peace in fluttering.
In every gust, a gentle sway,
Naps in the cyclone lead the way.

When calm returns, the world will pause,
Nature's beauty holds us, no flaws.
In the eye, we rest and breathe,
In swirling peace, our souls believe.

Flowing Through the Night

Whispers of the night breeze fade,
Stars twinkle softly, an endless parade.
Moonlit paths in silver weave,
Dreams awaken, take their leave.

Shadows dance in quiet grace,
Time stands still in this sacred space.
The world outside begins to yawn,
As night unveils its velvet dawn.

Crickets sing a lullaby sweet,
Nature's chorus, gentle and fleet.
With every breath, the silence deepens,
In the night's embrace, our spirit strengthens.

Flowing through this tranquil scene,
Moments linger, serene and keen.
Embrace the stillness, hold it tight,
In the magic of the flowing night.

Ribbons of Rest

In the hush of evening's glow,
Softly falls the velvet snow.
Time unwinds, a gentle thread,
Weaves a blanket, soothing bed.

Whispers of a sweet refrain,
Memories like an autumn rain.
Floating softly, dreams take flight,
Cradled in the arms of night.

Ribbons tied in slumber's bliss,
Every moment, a tender kiss.
Close your eyes, let worries cease,
In the depths, find perfect peace.

So let the world fade away,
In this embrace, forever stay.
For in the quiet, hearts will rest,
And find their calm in nature's nest.

The Magic of Gentle Gales

Whispers linger on the air,
Soft caresses, light as prayer.
Through the trees, the breezes glide,
Nature's song, a gentle ride.

Every leaf a dance, a sway,
Carrying thoughts where dreams may play.
In the fields, a soft refrain,
Echoes sweet like falling rain.

Magic stirs in every breath,
Life renewed through calm and depth.
Hold the winds, let worries pass,
In their arms, find peace at last.

So let the gentle gales unfold,
Stories whispered, dreams retold.
In this moment, let it be,
Nature's love, a symphony.

Daydreams on a Whirl

Thoughts take flight on gentle wings,
In the mind where freedom sings.
Colors swirl, a vibrant show,
Imagination's ebb and flow.

Caught in moments, fresh and bright,
Lost in daydreams, pure delight.
Like the clouds on summer's tide,
Wanders freely, open wide.

Twist and turn, the world a blur,
Every thought begins to stir.
Chasing visions, sweet and clear,
In the daydream, nothing to fear.

Round and round, the thoughts will twine,
In this dance, our hearts align.
Daydreams linger, soft and fair,
A swirling world, beyond compare.

Soaring into Solace

Upward I glide on whispered dreams,
Through skies of azure, where sunlight gleams.
Soft clouds embrace, like a gentle friend,
In this quiet flight, my worries suspend.

With wings of hope, I rise and sway,
In the warmth of peace, I drift away.
The world below, a distant sound,
As I find my heart in solace profound.

Each breath a note in the tranquil tune,
Beneath the vast, inviting moon.
I soar through realms of calm and grace,
In the light of the stars, I find my place.

Here I linger, in blissful flight,
Soaring into solace, a pure delight.
The spirit lifts, the heart knows well,
Content in the quiet, where dreams dwell.

Soft Heights of Serenity

In the distance, the mountains call,
Cloaked in whispers, they cradle all.
The air is sweet, a golden balm,
In soft heights, I find my calm.

Petals dance in the gentle breeze,
Nature's lullaby that aims to please.
Under the shade of ancient trees,
Life's worries fade, it's time to seize.

Sunlight drips through leaves like gold,
Tales of peace endlessly told.
In this haven, my heart takes flight,
In soft heights of serenity, I feel right.

With each step, the world unwinds,
In harmony with the peace that binds.
A tapestry woven of sighs and dreams,
In this tranquil space, nothing seems as it seems.

The Silent Merry-Go-Round

Round and round, the world spins slow,
In shades of twilight, the soft winds blow.
Each horse a story, each turn a sigh,
Under the stars, where memories lie.

Children laughing, a distant sound,
In the gentle grip of the merry-go-round.
Time stands still as the night wraps tight,
The moon observes, bathing all in light.

Familiar faces, lost in the bright,
Spinning dreams under soft moonlight.
A carousel of moments, sweet and clear,
The silent song that only hearts hear.

In this quiet dance, I close my eyes,
Floating softly, beneath velvet skies.
Finding joy in the spin and sway,
On the silent merry-go-round, I'll stay.

Breathe of the Sweet Zephyr

On the edge of dawn, the whispers wake,
A breath of the sweet zephyr, dreams to take.
It carries tales through the open fields,
In nature's arms, the heart gently yields.

Softly it sings to the bending trees,
Inlingering moments, timeless peace.
I follow the path where the wind will lead,
In whispers of flowers, my soul is freed.

The sky blushes pink with the softest touch,
While time flows gently, not hasty or rush.
Each inhale a gift from the waiting earth,
In this serene space, I find rebirth.

With every breeze, I know I belong,
In the dance of the zephyr, I sing my song.
In harmony found, my spirit will soar,
Breathe of the sweet zephyr, forevermore.

Sails of the Sleepy Sea

Beneath the twilight's gentle glow,
The sails are cast, a soft, sweet flow.
Whispers of waves in lullabies,
As moonlight dances in the skies.

Crickets sing in silent tune,
While stars adorn the velvet moon.
Drifting dreams on breezes light,
The sleepy sea, a soothing sight.

With every shift, the ship sways slow,
Carried forth where heartbeats go.
Embraced by night, so warm and deep,
The world around may gently sleep.

In this haven, time stands still,
Cradled by nature's tender will.
The sails now whisper soft and free,
In harmony with the sleepy sea.

Euphoria on the Edge

At the crest where shadows meet,
A thrill of joy, a pulse, a beat.
The wind rushes, wild and bold,
A dance of fire, a story told.

Sunrise paints the horizon bright,
With colors bold, a pure delight.
Each moment hangs, a fleeting spark,
Euphoria ignites the dark.

With daring hearts on paths unknown,
We chase the dreams that feel like home.
The edge is where we dare to leap,
Into the depths, a promise to keep.

Fingers reach for skies so vast,
Holding tight to moments cast.
In this embrace, we'll always glide,
Euphoria as our faithful guide.

The Calm After the Storm

The winds have hushed, the skies clear blue,
A world reborn, fresh and new.
Raindrops linger on the leaves,
A quiet hush, as nature breathes.

Clouds retreat, revealing light,
The golden sun, a gentle sight.
Birds return to joyous flight,
In the calm, all feels just right.

Puddles form, reflections gleam,
Nature whispers, soft as a dream.
In every corner, hope takes bloom,
The calm emerges from the gloom.

Now hearts are light, the past set free,
From chaos springs tranquility.
In this moment, life adorned,
We find our peace, reborn, transformed.

Cascading into Dreams

Moonlit rivers weave and flow,
Where softly winds and shadows glow.
A tapestry of night unfolds,
In whispers sweet, the heart beholds.

Stars above drip silvery beams,
Inviting all to float in dreams.
Each thought a petal, light as air,
Cascading visions, free of care.

Clouds like feathers drift away,
As nightingale sings to end the day.
In this realm where fantasies play,
Our burdens lift, our worries sway.

Embrace the night, let spirits soar,
Into the depths where dreams explore.
Cascading softly, hearts will gleam,
Awake at last, inside the dream.

Soundscapes of Sleep

In the hush of night it calls,
Soft murmurs cradle tender dreams.
Whispers weave through shadowed halls,
As moonlight paints gentle beams.

Stars hum a lullaby sweet,
Crickets sing in rhythmic flight.
A blanket of calm, so complete,
Guides us toward the depths of night.

Clouds drift like ships on a sea,
Guided by the softest breeze.
In this realm, we're wild and free,
Held in the twilight's warm ease.

Time pauses, a sighing breath,
In soundscapes woven from dreams.
Here, we flirt with gentle death,
Where silence is both light and gleams.

The Tempest's Embrace

In shadows deep, the thunder roars,
Lightning flashes, a wild dance.
Winds howl through the open doors,
Nature's wild and fierce romance.

Rain strikes down with heavy grace,
Each drop a note in darkened skies.
Chaos wraps us in its embrace,
While whispers of the storm arise.

Trees sway like dancers lost in time,
Roots hold tight, defiant and bold.
Through this tempest, hearts do chime,
In the storm's heart, stories unfold.

Lightning fades, the calm returns,
Yet in our souls, the fire burns.
From chaos, peace inevitably earns,
And in the heart, a lesson learns.

Nightfall's Whirl

As day gives way, the dusk unfurls,
A canvas painted deep and wide.
Whispers twirl in nature's swirls,
Gathering dreams, like the tide.

Cool breezes kiss the day goodbye,
Stars awaken, one by one.
In twilight's arms, we start to fly,
Bathed in hues of the setting sun.

The world drapes in velvet night,
Soft shadows dance, a gentle play.
Each silence swells, a pure delight,
And hopes drift high, like dreams astray.

In the night, our worries fade,
As time drifts softly with the moon.
In the stillness, peace is made,
And hearts begin to hum a tune.

Drowsy Whispers of the Wind

Gentle breezes call our names,
Through fields of golden dreams they glide.
Softly hum like distant flames,
Carrying secrets far and wide.

They whisper tales of lost desire,
Of places where the heart can soar.
In every sigh, a flickering fire,
Binding souls forevermore.

As twilight falls, the whispers grow,
Like silken threads through starlit skies.
In drowsy tones, they ebb and flow,
A lullaby for weary eyes.

Breath in their soft, inviting song,
For in their embrace, we find our peace.
In the night, where we belong,
Drowsy whispers coax us to release.

Cascades of Curiosity

Whispers of wonders call out to me,
Secrets in shadows, so hard to see.
A world full of questions, waiting to bloom,
With every new thought, dispelling the gloom.

Winding through forests of dreams and delight,
Where starlit paths glimmer, so lonely yet bright.
Each turn a new chapter, unfurled with a sigh,
Awakening wonders that never say die.

Rivers of thought, flowing fast and free,
Currents of knowledge, enticing the key.
Embrace the unknown, let your heart be your guide,
Adventures await on the turbulent tide.

In cascades of questions, the heart finds its voice,
Each ripple and echo, a vibrant choice.
Curiosity dances, with grace and with flair,
Leading us onward, beyond all compare.

The Dance of Drowsiness

A blanket of dreams wraps the world so tight,
As stars softly whisper, bidding goodnight.
In the hush of the evening, shadows will sway,
While the moon stretches lazily, drifting away.

With eyes gently closing, thoughts start to twirl,
Lost in the currents of sleep's tender whirl,
Where time bends and bows, in rhythm it weaves,
The dance of drowsiness, cradle of leaves.

Soft sighs of the night blend with echoes so sweet,
Each heartbeat a pulse in this rhythmic retreat.
Floating on clouds made of wishes and peace,
Where troubles dissolve and the worries decrease.

In twilight's embrace, let your spirit unwind,
As dreams come alive, in the stillness, combined.
The dance of drowsiness, gentle and slow,
Drifts through the cosmos, like soft falling snow.

Enchanted Vortex

In the heart of the forest, a whirlpool of light,
Sparkling with magic, alive in the night.
Whispers of ancients entwined with the trees,
Awaken our spirits, like the softest breeze.

Colors blend softly, twirling in space,
A canvas of wonders, each hue a grace.
In this enchanted vortex, reality bends,
Where dreams meet the dawn and the journey transcends.

Time dances with shadows, both fleeting and bright,
Embraced by the echoes of soft starry light.
Let wonder engulf you, as you spiral around,
In this realm of illusion, new magic is found.

Boundless horizons, where thoughts intertwine,
In the depths of the vortex, our hearts must align.
Each breath, a connection, each thought, a new thread,
In this enchanted vortex, where visions are fed.

Reverie in the Breeze

Gentle caresses of whispers float by,
A symphony played on the wings of the sky.
Xylophones tinkling in soft, tender air,
Awaking the senses, both vivid and rare.

In moments of stillness, thoughts take their flight,
Carried by breezes that dance through the night.
Where dreams massage edges of sleep's cool embrace,
And wander through corridors, time cannot trace.

Floating through valleys where laughter unfolds,
The reverie dances, as secrets are told.
With each gust of wonder, believe in your heart,
That breezes of magic will never depart.

In whispers, they linger, the echoes remain,
Reminding us gently of joy and of pain.
Reverie in the breeze, a sweet fleeting thrill,
Awakening memories that time cannot still.

Scented Breezes at Dawn

The sun peeks over the hills,
Awakening flowers with grace.
Gentle whispers fill the air,
Scented breezes start to chase.

Birds take flight in pastel skies,
Melodies weave through the trees.
Every moment wrapped in calm,
Nature breathes with tender ease.

Morning dew on blades of grass,
Sparkles bright with new day's glow.
Peaceful thoughts drift on the wind,
As warmth begins to flow.

A new day fresh as it seems,
Hope unfolds like petals wide.
In this tranquil, fragrant morn,
The heart opens, freed with pride.

Twilight's Turbulence

The sky ignites in fiery hues,
A dance of chaos up above.
Shadows stretch as day bids adieu,
An orchestra of distant love.

Clouds swirl in a bracing play,
Lightning flickers, nature's spark.
Whispers gather, night holds sway,
A symphony in the dark.

Winds carry secrets through the trees,
Branches sway in wild delight.
The horizon bleeds with memories,
As twilight unveils the night.

Stars emerge, a world reborn,
In chaos, beauty finds its way.
Twilight holds both peace and storm,
An embrace of night and day.

Restful Whirlpools

Gentle waters cradle dreams,
Rippling softly in the light.
Time slips by in gentle streams,
Whirlpools echo silent night.

Reflections dance on liquid glass,
Whispers blend with nature's sigh.
Every moment seems to pass,
In restful pools where hopes lie.

Leaves drift down like whispered thoughts,
Floating softly, held in grace.
In stillness, the heart is sought,
Restful whirlpools, warm embrace.

In the calm, a world unwinds,
Every breath is peace distilled.
In these depths, true solace finds,
The soul's quiet, soft and thrilled.

Elysian Gales

Winds from realms beyond the known,
Carry tales of distant lands.
In their touch, the seeds are sown,
Magic flows through unseen hands.

Rustling leaves in harmony,
A chorus sings of ancient lore.
Elysian gales, wild and free,
Whisper truths that life has store.

Clouds are painted in sunset's light,
Colors blending, pure delight.
Each gust holds a promise bright,
Of dreams awakened by the night.

Feel the breath of worlds long gone,
A gentle sway in every breath.
In these gales, our spirits drawn,
Finding life beyond all death.

Spirals of the Sublime

In shadows dance the stars so bright,
Whispers of the cosmos' light.
Each twirl wraps time in tight embrace,
Infinite dreams in boundless space.

Echoes of a lost refrain,
Softly calls through joy and pain.
Celestial notes in gentle sway,
Guide our hearts, come what may.

A spiral curve, a breath of air,
Lifts us high from earthly care.
In this place where spirits gleam,
Find our hopes, pursue the dream.

With every turn, a tale unfolds,
Of sacred truths the heart beholds.
In the dance of night and day,
Sublime arcs lead us away.

Driftwood Dreams

Upon the shore, they weave and sway,
Stories of the sea's long play.
Each piece of wood, a tale untold,
Carried by waves, in salt and gold.

Under the sun's warm, gentle kiss,
Whispers of the ocean's bliss.
Tangled roots of ancient trees,
Float on currents, ride the breeze.

In twilight's glow, reflections gleam,
Gathered hopes and driftwood dreams.
Nature's art, a masterpiece,
In every grain, a sense of peace.

When the night unveils its shroud,
Stars emerge, both bright and loud.
Through silvery moonlight, we roam,
Finding solace, discovering home.

Gale of Whimsy

A whirlwind spins with joyous glee,
Catching laughter from the trees.
Tickling leaves as they twirl high,
Underneath the bright blue sky.

With every gust, a story plays,
In the depths of childhood days.
Imagination takes its flight,
In the breeze, dreams feel so light.

Colors dance like butterflies,
Unfolding wings through happy sighs.
The gale brings whispers from afar,
Beneath the canopy of stars.

In whimsy's grasp, we joyously spin,
Lost in the play, our hearts begin.
To weave a tale through air so free,
In the whirl of a wild jubilee.

Nocturnal Whirlies

In the hush of night, shadows creep,
Dreamers roam while the world sleeps.
Silver light and secrets combine,
In the calm of the midnight's design.

Whirlies twirl in the pale moon's glare,
Painting stories in the crisp air.
With gentle nudges from the stars,
They dance through dreams, they wander far.

A tapestry of laughter, sighs,
Flecked with joy and soft goodbyes.
In twilight's charm, we lose our way,
On paths where whispered wishes play.

Nocturnal magic fills the night,
Guiding hearts to endless flight.
From shadows deep, a glimmering spark,
Awakens dreams hidden in the dark.

Echoes of the Windy Dreamer

In whispers soft the breezes flow,
They carry tales from long ago.
A heart that wanders, seeking light,
In shadows deep, it finds its flight.

Beneath the stars, where dreams unwind,
The echoes dance, the stars aligned.
Through fields of gold, with hope we chase,
The spirit's call, a warm embrace.

With each gust, a story spun,
Of journeys had, of battles won.
The dreamer smiles, as night consumes,
In silence rich, where magic blooms.

And thus we drift on winds so free,
In echo's song, we find our key.
A melody of dreams displayed,
In twilight's arms, we are remade.

Celestial Twirls of Delight

A dance of stars in velvet skies,
In twirls of light, the cosmos flies.
The moonlight weaves a gossamer thread,
In heartbeats soft, our dreams are fed.

Around the sun, the planets glide,
In harmony, they soar and bide.
With every spin, a story told,
Of fiery hearts, in warmth they fold.

The universe hums a gentle tune,
In cosmic swirls, we are marooned.
Delight cascades in twinkling beats,
Where time and space in beauty meet.

And as we watch the heavens play,
We find our hearts in soft array.
Celestial whims, so pure and bright,
In every twirl, our spirits' flight.

Lullabies on the Horizon

The sun dips low, a painted sky,
With whispers soft as night draws nigh.
A lullaby of waves will hum,
As dreams awaken, shadows come.

In twilight's arms, the world subsides,
As hope and calm in stillness hides.
The stars ignite, a gentle spark,
And all the worries fade to dark.

With moonlit paths and soft caress,
The heart finds peace, a sweet recess.
In lullabies that kiss the shore,
We drift away, forevermore.

So close your eyes, let dreams take flight,
On horizons vast, through endless night.
A song of love, of sweet repose,
Forever in the heart it grows.

Twists of Tranquility

In stillness found, the water flows,
With gentle curves the river knows.
A quiet path where peace will lead,
In every twist, the heart is freed.

Amid the trees, where silence reigns,
The breath of earth removes the chains.
With every leaf, a secret shared,
In whispered tones, the journey bared.

The twilight hums a soothing song,
In nature's lap, we all belong.
As shadows stretch and daylight wanes,
A tranquil heart, love still remains.

In quiet corners, hope will bloom,
Where peace resides, dispelling gloom.
Through every twist, tranquility,
In harmony, the soul feels free.

Hushed Currents of Bliss

In the quiet of the night,
Soft whispers gently flow,
Carried by the moon's light,
Where secret joys can grow.

A serene river glistens,
Reflecting stars like dreams,
Each ripple softly listens,
To heart's unspoken themes.

Gentle breezes caress,
As time begins to freeze,
In the depths of the heavens,
Lies a tranquil ease.

Blissful moments unfold,
In the hush of the air,
With stories yet untold,
In this peaceful prayer.

Whirling Leaves of Imagination

Leaves dance in the breeze,
Spinning tales of yore,
Chasing dreams with ease,
On the forest floor.

Colors blend and swirl,
A canvas in the air,
Imagined worlds unfurl,
In a playful flair.

Each twirl sparks a thought,
A journey to explore,
In every twist and knot,
Endless paths to soar.

Nature's art displayed,
In a waltz of delight,
Where shadows serenade,
And the heart takes flight.

Tidal Waves of Tranquility

In the dusk, waves hush,
Kissing the sandy shore,
With a gentle rush,
That beckons for more.

Swells of peace arise,
Breathing calm and serene,
Under vast blue skies,
Where the soul can glean.

Each tide brings a sigh,
A balm for weary minds,
Washing worries by,
In the ebb that binds.

Stillness spreads like foam,
In the fading light's glow,
Here, the heart finds home,
In the waves' soft flow.

Dizziness of Delight

A whirlwind of laughter,
Spinning fast in the air,
Chasing joy hereafter,
Without a single care.

Fleeting moments gleam,
As time begins to blur,
In a vibrant dream,
Where happiness can stir.

Colors dance and play,
In an endless embrace,
Creating a new day,
In a radiant space.

Lost in playful spins,
Where worries disappear,
Let the merry wins,
Fill the heart with cheer.

Euphoria of the Evening Storm

The sky ignites in vibrant hue,
As thunder rumbles deep and true.
Raindrops dance on thirsty ground,
A symphony of joy is found.

With every flash, a heartbeat stirs,
The world transformed, the mind concurs.
Nature's breath, a wild embrace,
In storm's chaos, we find grace.

The scent of earth, rejuvenation,
In every drop, a celebration.
The evening glows with electric thrill,
As shadows flicker, hearts stand still.

In this moment, time suspends,
Euphoria sings as daylight ends.
A canvas painted in the storm,
Where wild and tender hearts are warm.

Serendipity in the Swirl

In a whirl of colors, joy appears,
Life's little quirks, beyond the years.
Every turn, a chance to see,
The beauty wrapped in mystery.

A fleeting glance, a smile shared,
In crowded streets, the soul declared.
Moments weave like threads of gold,
Serendipity, a tale retold.

Twist and twirl, take a chance,
In life's dance, we take our stance.
Unexpected paths ignite the heart,
From chaos blooms the finest art.

Each stumble leads to new delight,
In every shadow, there's a light.
The swirl of life, a wondrous spin,
In serendipity, we begin.

Storms of Serenity

In the hush before the rain,
Whispers linger, soft refrain.
Clouds gather with a gentle hum,
A prelude where calm will succumb.

When winds rise high and spirits soar,
Nature's heartbeat, wild and more.
Lightning dances, brief and bright,
In the chaos, we seek light.

Amidst the storm, a tranquil space,
Where chaos meets a warm embrace.
Waves crash strong, yet peace resounds,
In storms of calm, our soul is found.

As skies clear, the sunset sings,
Rebirth emerges with the wings.
Through storms of life, serenity flows,
In every tempest, wonder grows.

Dreamscapes in Motion

In twilight's glow, the dreams take flight,
A ballet born in soft moonlight.
Whispers of wishes, softly drift,
In the silence, spirits lift.

Visions dance on starlit streams,
Reality fades as we chase dreams.
Every heartbeat, a thread of fate,
In dreamscapes, we create.

Wander through the shadows deep,
In secret places, our hearts leap.
Color the night with imagined grace,
In every dream, we find our place.

Together we weave, hand in hand,
In motion's flow, a gentle strand.
From dreams to life, we take the chance,
In dreamscapes, we learn to dance.

Whispers of the Sleeping Sky

Beneath the stars, the silence breathes,
A lullaby in soft moonbeams.
Dreams sail by on gentle waves,
In stillness, night's sweet secret weaves.

Clouds drift slow, like thoughts that roam,
Embracing souls, far away from home.
The breeze carries whispers of old,
In the patter of dreams, stories unfold.

In darkness, the shadows play a game,
Each flicker of light a spark, a flame.
As starlit eyes begin to close,
The heart finds peace where silence flows.

Wait for dawn, the night gently sighs,
With tender hugs from the sleeping skies.
Each twinkle a promise, soft and bright,
Inviting us back to the quiet night.

Twirling Tales of the Night

In the hush, secrets twirl and spin,
Whispered stories beneath the skin.
Moonlit dances in shadowed grace,
Fragments of dreams, a timeless chase.

Stars gather round, their light takes flight,
Weaving wonders in the velvet night.
A tale is born with every breeze,
Air thick with magic, a moment's tease.

Echoes of laughter, laughter so bright,
Painted lightly in shades of the night.
With each twirl, a memory calls,
The night is alive as the evening falls.

Let your heart dance wherever it may,
In the embrace of night, find your way.
For in every turn, a journey awaits,
Twirling tales open magical gates.

Cyclones of Imagination

Whirling thoughts take daring flight,
Spinning dreams in the canvas of night.
A tempest brews in the mind's eye,
Where visions soar and moments fly.

Colors collide in a vibrant swirl,
Ideas burst forth, they twist and twirl.
Each cyclone carries a story's seed,
Planting the hopes of tomorrow's need.

Spirals of wonder, vast and deep,
In swirling winds, our passions leap.
Crafting worlds that shimmer and shine,
In the heart of storms, the treasures align.

Ride the gales of your wildest dreams,
Find solace beneath the moonlit beams.
For in the chaos, creation is found,
Cyclones of imagination spin all around.

Slumber's Soft Embrace

In the quiet, where dreams reside,
Slumber whispers, arms open wide.
A sanctuary wrapped in night's shawl,
With tender comfort that beckons all.

Softly it calls, a warm, sweet song,
Where restless minds finally belong.
Each heartbeat slows, the world stands still,
In slumber's embrace, our hearts begin to fill.

The brain learns to dance, in gentle sway,
As worries fade, they drift away.
Wrapped in soft layers, cocooned in peace,
In this soothing space, all troubles cease.

So close your eyes, let the day unfurl,
In the arms of sleep, let magic swirl.
For in slumber, we find our grace,
Forever held in soft embrace.

Cascade of Dreams

In twilight's glow, the rivers flow,
Whispers of hope in silver skies.
Each ripple sings, as time swings slow,
Through glistening realms where spirit flies.

Mountains stand tall, their shadows dance,
Guardians of secrets, timeless and wise.
In nature's embrace, we're lost in a trance,
Where every thought, like water, sighs.

Stars above gleam, a celestial stream,
Carving our paths in darkness bright.
We chase the echoes of every dream,
In the heart of the quiet night.

This cascade flows, with stories untold,
Of wishes made beneath the moon.
In every drop, a memory bold,
Where faded hopes and visions bloom.

The Sound of Breezes

Gentle whispers through the leaves,
A song of peace as daylight weaves.
Each breath of wind, a soft caress,
Nature's kiss, a sweet, warm press.

Clouds drift by in skies so blue,
The breeze carries tales anew.
A rustling chorus, pure delight,
Echoes of joy take wing in flight.

As flowers sway, they join the dance,
Swaying gently in a trance.
The world awakens, spirits lift,
In the breeze, we find our gift.

Listen closely, hear the sound,
Of dreams released, a love unbound.
In every gust, a heart reborn,
The sacred breath of the morn.

Fantasies in the Storm

Thunder rumbles, fierce and loud,
Dark clouds gather, a brooding shroud.
Lightning flashes, a fleeting spark,
Illuminating dreams in the dark.

Rain dances down, a wild ballet,
Each drop a promise, washing grey.
In the tempest, we find our flight,
Fantasies awaken, igniting the night.

Voices roar in nature's symphony,
Echoing deep, a primal harmony.
Whirling winds, they twist and turn,
In the storm's embrace, we learn.

From chaos, beauty starts to rise,
As hope peeks through the weeping skies.
In every storm, a tale is spun,
Of dreams set free, the journey begun.

Windswept Dreamscapes

Amid the dunes, the landscapes shift,
Windswept visions, a gentle lift.
In golden grains, our thoughts take flight,
Chasing shadows in soft twilight.

Mountains erase in the swirling air,
Each grain a whisper of secrets rare.
Footprints fade, as echoes blend,
In this vast realm where dreams transcend.

Soft breezes carry our hopes afar,
Guided by the light of a wandering star.
In these dreamscapes, we lose our ways,
Joyfully adrift in endless rays.

Yet in this dance, we find our grace,
As winds embrace our souls in space.
Here, in solace, our hearts awake,
In windswept realms, no walls can break.

Milton Keynes UK
Ingram Content Group UK Ltd.
UKHW020735301124
451807UK00019B/788